GW00708391

danieldrechmist.com

WRECK OF THE JEANNE GOUGY

*for Jenny*

To Linda

Best wishes

[signature] 2 Sept. 2001

and best wishes too

from Daniel

# Wreck of the Jeanne Gougy

Colin Pink

*with illustrations by*
Daniel Goodwin

Paekakariki Press

2021

ISBN: 9781908133434

*Acknowledgements*
Many thanks to the editors of the following publications
where some of the poems previously appeared: *Poetry
Salzburg Review; The Cannon's Mouth; Ink Sweat and Tears;
Poetry Wivenhoe.*

Typeset in 12pt 'Monotype' Garamond 156

Printed at Paekakariki Press
Walthamstow
2021

paekakarikipress.com

# Contents

## *Sylvia Plath on the Moor, September 1956*

She is a sylph punctuation mark on the horizon;
perched on top a dry stone wall, one foot dangling
among the cowslips, the other crossed to create
a makeshift desk to balance her portable typewriter.

Absorbed in her writing she is outside yet really
she's inside all along and seems oblivious to the rough
charm of the Yorkshire moors, whose flora and fauna
lie mostly hidden behind a dour unpredictable mist.

She is not far from Top Withens, the ruined house
claimed to be the inspiration for Wuthering Heights.
Perhaps there is still a ghostly whisper on the air.

Sylvia has married her own Heathcliff whose voice
she thought was like the thunder of God, each syllable
as precise and weighty as the stones on which she sits.

# Fragments from the Croc's Mouth

Sappho, I thought you should know, your love poems,
long thought lost, turned up at last, shredded into thin
strips, in the mummified corpse of a crocodile. That's
what I call style! The elusive gaps in your verse make
an even greater yearning than a complete redaction.
That's just like love, to sit in the gap between giver
and receiver, filling the void with promised treasure,
leaving us orbiting a star that sucks us ever nearer.

Love, I seek          your distinctive gait,          gesture,
          lost profile                    out of reach, enticing
     follow in   shadows. How many     tongues
must I taste in search of you? Talking on the phone I can't
stop      pacing,          a dog circling ever tighter the length
of its tether,          on the scent of          contentment.

# Pont des Arts

On this bridge lovers fasten padlocks
to declare they are joined together.
How sad the beat of those steel hearts.
How many have since broken apart?
Imagery of enchainment betrays fears
of being shackled together for eternity.
How many regret passion's hasty clasp,
wish they hadn't thrown away the key?

Love is the breeze that tickles the hairs
along your arm as you cross the bridge
and tingles when you meet, it's invisible,
changeable, yet so tangible you taste it.
Bend with the wind, flex apart and back,
that way the sapling of love won't snap.

## Thanatos and Eros

Thanatos came knocking at the door
I said he must have the wrong address
He turned away but on the next day
Like a Jehovah's Witness knocked again.
He'd brought some texts on mortality
And invited me to attend a free event
Where everything would be explained
And any doubts allayed. I thanked him
And said I'd think about it but I was
Rather busy just now. He warned me
About a confidence trickster, known as
Eros. Advised me not to open the door.
I thanked him for his concern and left
The door off the latch. It's never too late.

# Breakfast with the Birds 1934

*after Das Frühstück der Vögel 1934 by Gabriele Münter*

There's snow on the trees beyond the window
and the birds, robins and goldfinches, perch
on the boughs. You sit, solitary, at breakfast
before the window, commune with the birds.
You and the birds share your frugal frühstück;
everything is poised, in its place, the plate on the
table, snow on the bough, the coffeepot's jaunty
spout, your calm back as you watch the birds.

And everything not of this moment evaporates;
you watch and wait; the birds watch and wait;
and the world holds its breath as long as it takes.
The thrum of the real, the hardness of the table,
the transparency of the window glass, and on
your tongue the peculiar flavour of this instant.

## *Summer Gales Sennen Cove*

Summer gales turn our tent into a drunken boat;
the canvas yaws, riding gusts that pull it about
like toddlers fighting over a toy, until I think
we'll surely sink, hull shredded, and crawl out
from under flapping waves of damp canvas.
We're battered senseless by the storm's invisible
blows whose racket is unrelenting, preventing
sleep or comfort with its all night club-clubbing.

The radio clings to a thin signal, rising and fading,
offering sips of orchestral succour while the rain
lands on the canvas like blows from a cat-of-nine;
by the third day we begin to take it personally,
believe a nature God, offended by our trespass,
is out to teach us a lesson that we won't forget.

## Night-Time

Who needs sleep? It drowns
the night in dreams, rummages
in the mind-midden for lost
treasure that turns out to be
incessant tales told by an idiot;
a voice muttering to itself with
the scribble-scrabble of unbidden
recollection gnawing at the night.

It's a strange gift, the hours of 2 to 4
when night scratches its spells into
the page of silence and the hands
of the clock unmask the pace of time
and sharp quills write in secret ink
the twisted logic of our lives.

## *Youth*

Untimely, it runs through fingers, swift as water;
the fragile cup our hands make are no container
fit enough for a journey longer than between,
say, a mountain stream and our lips. There's
always that elusive sparkle, things that slip
from our grasp, lit by a light fastened from within
that dazes us, amazes us, with prismatic flowers
beneath our feet. High above unfurls a canopy
of iridescent blooms, cloud painted, air-brushed
across the sky, leaving impressions locked in
the dressing up box of memories, to be tried on
one more time, as day learns to embrace the dark,
listen to the beat of owl's wings, destined to bring
messages from Minerva that never arrive in time.

# William Mills (Inventor) 1856-1932

I see you, bent over your desk, drawing
the pineapple skin casing of a Mills Bomb.
You rule fine technical lines, engineering
exactly each part, so that it will ripen on
cue, when the charge goes off, splinter into
many ragged parts, that in their burning
haste tear jagged wounds in anyone who
is in the way; a field of poppies flowering.

Seventy-five million of these little iron hunks
were made. That's a whole lot of hot metal.
Let us collect up the fragments: the chunks
of flesh, splinters of bone, the slippery offal,
served in a rich red sauce in recurring dreams
accompanied by a vintage bottle of screams.

# The White Rose

*i.m. members of the White Rose German resistance movement 1942-1943*

To think when thought is forbidden.
To love when taught to hate.
To resist the surge of the crowd.
To manœuvre in a world of control.
To speak when silence is enforced.
To question when orders are the norm.
To look the tyrant in the eye and defy.
To dream of peace in a world of war.
To cradle hope newborn in your arms.
To feel the undertow and keep swimming.
To wait for the knock on the door.
To listen to the scrape of gaolers' keys.
To face down the ranting judge.
To listen for the drop of the blade.

# Sophie's Dream

*i.m. Sophie Scholl 9 May 1921–22 February 1943*

You carry the infant close to you—careful not to fall;
wrapped in a shawl gazing out at the world the baby's
unfocussed eyes absorb the blur of everything. Hands
with tiny transparent fingernails on tiny fingers flex
the air. It's a fine sunny day, almost festive, as you climb
up the steep track to the church that stands crag-like
in its mountainous home. Its wind-battered stones
make a retreat for those seeking refuge from the storm.

Before you a crevasse opens in slack jawed brutality;
its slippery edge gapes between you and your refuge;
an icy breath freezes all motion as you get nearer.
Just in time you place the child on the other side;
it lies among the flourishing buds of the future
but it is too late for you and you fall into the abyss.

This poem is based on the dream Sophie Scholl had the
night before her execution on 22 February 1943 for her role
in the White Rose anti-Nazi resistance movement in Munich.

# Job Application

*Found poem based on letters by the philosopher Rush Rhees*

Notwithstanding the opportunities furnished to me
and the time I have allowed myself I've succeeded
neither in preparing anything for publication nor in
completing a thesis for a PhD. Nor can I see any great
likelihood of my doing so. I've applied for posts as
lecturer or assistant lecturer at three colleges. One
gave me an interview and dismissed me, the others
saw no need for an interview. My latest employment
has been as a shop assistant in a bookshop. In conclusion
I perhaps ought to say that I have serious doubts about
my competence in the sort of post I am applying for.
I like teaching and am interested in philosophy. But
I have not made an unqualified success of either, and
do not grow more sanguine with time. Yours Truly.

## *Wreck of the Jeanne Gougy*

        The clog of it;
      Water a stone in the throat;
    The gasp of it—outbursting
      *Oh God no not again!*
  The sweep and sway of it; the world tilting
Power of it, turning up to down, down to up.
    The childish jostle of it, barging in
Again and again, extinguishing air and light.

       The boat a mere toy;
      Flung this way and that;
    The disdainful waves breaking:
      *Oh God no not again!*
  Racing to the shore, oblivious of what lies
Before; unconcerned nature exercises her
    Sovereign power, flexes her muscles
To remind us how truly puny we really are.

       The Jeanne Gougy
     A trawler out of Dieppe
   Ran aground at Gamper Bay;
    *Chi Rho the sea reaps.*
  Sailing out from Waterford her belly full
Of fish, blinded by the storm, and swept
    Onto jagged teeth snapping at the sea
Capsized between Sennen Cove and Land's End.

The rollers rolled her
Over as if tripping an infant;
Trapped inside the crew gasp for breath:
*Oh God no not again!*
And the water races through her like keen
Customs men search for souls to impound
Do you have anything to declare?
Hurry now—the hour is later than you think.

The cliffs loom over her;
Provide balcony seats for this
The latest tragedy to be performed:
*Oh God no not again!*
Prayers are no use, snatched away by the wind
Like a sailor's cap tossed over the quay;
And all is illuminated by the parachute
Flares so that we might witness men wrestle waves.

The sailors are thrown
From side to side, collide
Battered by the fist of the storm
*Oh God no not again!*
On the cliff edge the rescuers watch, casual,
Uncannily calm in their perch above peril;
They stand, hands in pockets, and stare
As the bulwarks spew salt sea again and again.

The boat rolls over;
Surely no-one can survive inside?
Surf crashes over her in joyous possession:
*Chi Rho the sea reaps.*
Then a head emerges from the bridge balcony
Gasping between elements and hunched shoulders;
Rocket lines are fired towards the boat;
He reaches for them and is cursorily swept away.

The lines are fired again;
Snag on wire stays, but hold fast
At last in place; then comes another wave:
*Oh God no not again!*
The sea is a lion's paw, playing with its prey
Before gulping it down, crushed between implacable
Jaws that effortlessly chew up metal
And flesh and spits out the bones it can't digest.

The breeches buoy sways;
Thin wire and air all that saves
A fisherman from another incoming wave:
*Oh God no not again!*
The sailor dangles between cliff and abyss as the men
Haul him ashore and the trawler's carcass is ravaged;
A bone licked by the sea, broken by molars
That grind it down to suck out the tender marrow.

The fishermen crawl
Out of the bridge, stunned
By the ferocity of the deluge
*Oh God no not again!*
That never ceases from playing with them
Beyond any form of exhaustion, muscles
Burning like electric wires, throats
Raw from being stuffed by the salt thrust of the sea.

The Jeanne Gougy
Rolls over and up and over;
The wire sways, another man in need
*Oh God no not again!*
Crawls from the belly of the boat, the weak
Runt of a litter, just able to flop out into air
Air that must be snatched quickly
From the stiff-clasped purse of the storm.

The helicopter hovers;
From its belly spools out
A spider's silk; a man swaying on a wire.
*The sea is a restless soul*
And rises up as if to snatch the rescuer
From the air and drag him down to the wreck's
Belly already digesting men with
Sea filled lungs afloat in the boat to greet him.

The winch man
Dangles over death; ignores
The tempest clawing at his feet.
*The swell's might, the waves spite*
Judder and snap, rivets rattle and teeth jar and
The sea jabs, a swift boxer, at the staggering boat.
Two more fishermen are lifted
Off, actors ascending at the end of a miracle play.

The Jeanne Gougy
A trawler out of Dieppe
Ran aground at 5am 3rd November;
*Chi Rho the sea reaps.*
She was ground to pieces in the thew grip
Of the sea. It was 1962, of her crew twelve
Drowned, just six were rescued;
The Beach Boys had a hit with *Surfin' Safari*.

## Late Night Movie

We're trapped in a badly made disaster movie
Spring brings sprouting fear that's contagious
This invisible enemy is fought by an antibody
We're trapped in a badly made disaster movie
There will be late-night repeats before victory
No Bruce Willis character turns up to save us
We're trapped in a badly made disaster movie
Spring brings sprouting fear that's contagious

## Don't Look Back

Fate walks behind you but don't look back
For our destiny we are not allowed to see
To know how long we might be on the rack
Fate walks behind you but don't look back
It won't protect you from a sudden attack
Pick up the pace stride on as if you're free
Fate walks behind you but don't look back
For our destiny we are not allowed to see

## On Not Grasping the Plot

Like an old photograph left out in the sun
I feel my dreams slowly curl at the edges
Hope begins to fade and fall apart undone
Like an old photograph left out in the sun
The story was a mess before it was begun
The cast unlikely to attract lenient judges
Like an old photograph left out in the sun
I feel my dreams slowly curl at the edges


## Old Photographs

Family photos preserve our memories
Frozen in emulsion that slowly decays
Sepia ancestors and lost rural remedies
Family photos preserve our memories
Coating the past in misplaced reveries
Imagining a better place in the old days
Family photos preserve our memories
Frozen in emulsion that slowly decays

## Intersection

At the intersection is where we meet
Each crossing over to greet the other
Desire makes our conjunction sweet
At the intersection is where we meet
Our time together is precious but fleet
There are so many things to discover
At the intersection is where we meet
Each crossing over to greet the other


## Dancers

Hold out your hand and place it in mine
Together we'll fill our cup of emptiness
Spill out our dreams so they might align
Hold out your hand and place it in mine
And we shall dance together for all time
Cunningly snatch bliss from the abyss
Hold out your hand and place it in mine
Together we'll fill our cup of emptiness

## Stolen Moments

It was time stolen from the public calendar
Purloined from the grip of family and friends
An oasis of moments shared in one summer
It was time stolen from the public calendar
It was forbidden but filled us with pleasure
We overflowed ourselves but it had to end
It was time stolen from the public calendar
Purloined from the grip of family and friends


## Awaking

I did not realise until it was almost too late
Love needs nurturing like a tender flower
The best time is the morning's clean slate
I did not realise until it was almost too late
That our dreams often die before we awake
And our lives hurry towards the final hour
I did not realise until it was almost too late
Love needs nurturing like a tender flower

## Official History

Think of the lies that repose in history books
Creating the accepted story of every nation
Signatures bound in boards dark as rooks
Think of the lies that repose in history books
Truth an enfeebled voice easily overlooked
Losers' stories erased in the final redaction
Think of the lies that repose in history books
Creating the accepted story of every nation


## Lamentation by Käthe Kollwitz
*(in memory of Ernst Barlach, bronze, 1938)*

The grief is for you and the angels sigh
for these dark times. The grief is frozen
bronze clamped over our mouth and eyes.
The grief is for you and the angels sigh
and stretch strong arms up unto the sky
and ask who is saved and who is chosen?
The grief is for you and the angels sigh.
For these dark times the grief is frozen.